AF493218

Sophy Chen's First E-C Original Poetry Collection
苏菲首部英汉诗歌原创集

A Wizened Rose
枯萎的玫瑰

Language: English and Chinese Bilingual
语　言：英汉对照

Author: [China] Sophy Chen / Lihua Chen
作　者：[中国] 苏　菲 / 陈丽华

Chief Editor: [China] Sophy Chen / Lihua Chen
主　编：[中国] 苏　菲 / 陈丽华

Assitant Editor: [China] Dazang Chen
副主编：[中国] 大　藏

苏菲国际翻译出版社
Sophy International Translation Publishing House

CONTENTS 目录

Preface 自 序

Review 评 论

Poems From Sophy Chen's Original E-C Poetry Beijing Poetry Series
苏菲原创英汉诗歌 北京诗歌系列节选

Poems From Sophy Chen's Original E–C Poetry Hometown Poetry Series
苏菲原创英汉诗歌　故乡诗歌系列节选

Sophy Chen's Some Words Before A Wizened Rose Published

— Sophy Chen's First Original E-C Poetry Collection

[China] Sophy Chen

As an English and Chinese bilingual poet and poetry translator for many years, I've translated many poetry collections into English and published them as books in paper and even in 14 nations but I did not really publish my own English and Chinese bilingual poetry collection in paper till now. Having been pushed to publish my own poetry collections by poets from all over of the world years by years, especially forced by Seneca Prize of Italy this year, I will be awarded as its ambassador in Italy on stage and so I must take my own poetry collection to Italy and then I must publish my own poetry collection in paper before I go to Italy.

In such rush hours of me, now I do not know what I will say in front of my poetry collection, My First Original E-C Poetry Collection, A Wizened Rose, and I only feel so relaxed now because all of poems both in English and Chinese were edited in a printing book file by poet Dazang Chen and especially the cover of the book has been finished to design by him too, and thanks for his hard work and love.

In this book I chose 30 poems of me both in English and Chinese languages and some of them written in English first and then translated into Chinese by me and some of them in Chinese first and then translated into English by me and some poems written in English and Chinese at same time and among them some poems published on line and some poems not published on line both in English and Chinese.

A Wizened Rose, the whole book is divided into four parts. Sophy Chen's Original E-C Poetry Beijing Poetry Series; Sophy Chen's Original E-C Poetry Hometown Poetry Series; Sophy Chen's Original English Sonnets; Sophy Chen's Original E-C Poetry Xiaoguwei Island Poetry Series.

A Wizened Rose, is chosen from my Beijing Poetry Series, Original E-C Poetry. In this poetry series, I love this poem so much because it gives me a very good memory of life in Beijing, and in 2012-11-7, Yanjiao Beijing, China, it was a very cold winter and all of things outside of window nearly wizened in dried colors and in a choking smell with haze flying in the air and it is a miracle that the rose, a white rose, in a black vase, on my desk for poems translation wizened but it still emanates its fragrance. It is a great pity that I could not take a picture of the rose and the black vase, by a camera or a phone, the vase, actually not a real vast, it was a black red wine bottle, and it was coincidentally that it was in a very good match of the white rose at that time so I think white rose and black bottle match or not it is well based on your life style and your attitude of life and it is none of business of anything but your love of your own life. Now i have no regret that i have held its permanent beauty in my poem just like i have held my life with the rose, black vase and even him in my permanent poetry.

It is a poem in style of English Haiku and it is written in English and i translated it into Chinese years later. The English Haiku I learn to write from American poets, especially the American poet, Ron Chapman, who told me how to write English Haiku hand by hand and searched me so many information on Haiku writing skills, and he still taught me what is the difference of Japanese Haiku and South Korean Haiku in English language.

Now i need to thank Ron Chapman who taught me this wonderful English writing style and i need to thank that cold winter in Beijing too and of course i need to thank the man who gave me this precious rose as a gift and i must thank the black red wine bottle, the desk, the poetry, my poetry translation and even the poems of poets because without one of them, this poem, A Wizened Rose, can not be born in my life and in my poetry permanently and of course this poetry collection can not be created and published either.

According to Hometown Poetry Series, of my Original E-C Poetry, my Original English Sonnets and Xiaoguwei Island Poetry Series of Original E-C Poetry, i would like you read my poetry collection, A Wizened Rose, and all of my good poems in this book and thanks for your time of reading.

Sophy Chen 2023-09-30, Guangzhou, China.

苏菲写在《枯萎的玫瑰》出版前的几句话

——苏菲首部英汉诗歌原创集

[中国] 苏 菲

作为一名多年从事中英文双语诗歌翻译的诗人、翻译家，自己已将多部诗集翻译成英文或汉语，并出版了纸质版图书，甚至在 14 个国家出版发行，但直到现在，还没有真正出版过自己的纸质版中英文双语诗集。

世界各地的诗人年年都催着我出版自己的诗集，尤其是今年意大利的塞内卡诗歌奖更是迫使我不得不出版自己的纸质版诗集，我将在舞台上被授予意大利塞内卡诗歌奖驻华大使，因此必须把自己的诗集带到意大利去，在去意大利之前，必须出版自己的纸质诗集。

在如此繁忙、慌乱，措手不及的时刻，面对我的诗集，首部英汉诗歌原创集《枯萎的玫瑰》，我不知道该说些什么，我现在感到无比的放松，因为诗人大藏已经将本书所有的中英文诗编辑成可以直接印刷的文本，尤其是这本书的封面也由他设计完成了，感谢他的辛勤工作和爱。

这本诗集入选了我 30 首中英文原创诗歌，其中一些诗是用英文写的，后来我又翻译成汉语的，一些诗用汉语写的，后来我又翻译成英语的，还有一些诗是同时用英语和汉语写的。其中有些诗在网上中英文发表过，有些在网上还没有发表过。

《枯萎的玫瑰》全书分为四个部分。苏菲原创英汉诗歌北京诗歌系列节选、苏菲原创英汉诗歌故乡诗歌系列节选、苏菲原创英语十四诗节选、 苏菲原创英汉诗歌小谷围岛诗歌系列节选。

　　《枯萎的玫瑰》选自我的北京诗歌系列。在这个诗歌系列里，我最喜欢这首诗，因为它留给我在北京一个非常美好的记忆。2012-11-7 中国北京燕郊，这是一个非常寒冷的冬天，窗外的万事万物，几近枯萎，余留干枯的色调和令人窒息，雾霾横飞，呛人的气味。这简直是个奇迹，一只玫瑰，白玫瑰，一个黑色花瓶，放在我的书桌上，我翻译诗歌的桌子，它已经枯萎，干瘪，但仍然散发着淡淡的香味。很遗憾，我没能用相机或手机拍下这只白玫瑰和黑花瓶。花瓶，实际上并不是真正的花瓶，那是一个黑色的红酒瓶，巧合的是，彼时它和这只白玫瑰简直是绝配。因此我认为白玫瑰和黑色瓶子匹配与否是你的生活方式和你的生活态度决定的。你对自己生活的热爱无关任何事物。

　　现在我并无遗憾，因为我已经将它永恒的美保存在我的诗里，正如我把生命、玫瑰、黑花瓶、甚至是他保存在我永恒的诗里。

　　这是一首英语俳句风格的诗。原文是用英语写得，汉语是数年后我翻译的文本。我从美国诗人那里学来的英语俳句，尤其是美国诗人罗纳德·詹姆斯·查普曼。他告诉我如何写英语俳句，并为我搜索了很多关于俳句的写作技巧信息，他还教我日本俳句和韩国俳句在英语中的区别。

　　现在，我要感谢罗纳德·詹姆斯·查普曼，是他教会了我这种美妙的英文写作风格，我也要感谢北京那个寒冷的冬天，当然，我还要感谢送给我这朵珍贵玫瑰礼物的人，我还要感谢那个黑色的红酒瓶，那张桌子，诗歌，我的诗歌翻译，甚至诗人的诗歌，因为没有它们，这首诗《枯萎的玫瑰》不可能在我的生活和我的诗歌中永恒诞生，当然这本诗集也不可能创作和出版。

　　至于我的原创英汉诗歌故乡诗歌系列节选、原创英语十四诗节选、原创英汉诗歌小谷围岛诗歌系列节选，就请你读我的诗集《枯萎的玫瑰》，所有的好诗都在书里，感谢你不惜费时阅读。

2023-09-30 中国广州

从露珠到溪流，诗思明快向外的自然流露

——评苏菲首部英汉诗歌原创集《枯萎的玫瑰》

[中国] 大　藏

苏菲的这部英汉双语诗歌原创集《枯萎的玫瑰》，诗歌写作跨越了 11 年，时间跨度非常之大。要评价苏菲的英汉双语诗歌原创，并不是一件容易的事情。我作为她身边最亲近的人，最熟悉她的写作和诗歌。这些年她的英汉双语诗歌原创不断成熟和丰富，从白璧无瑕的英语十四行诗"晚香玉"上的露珠，蜕变成奔向真正诗歌海洋的溪流。她作为一位真正的诗人，也渐渐走向成熟、沉稳甚至大气，不可三言两语而论之。

首先，苏菲的英汉双语诗歌原创表现出格调、题材的多元化，呈现出作为一个成熟"诗人"的基本特征。可以这么说，她的诗歌从一开始，除了少数的几篇，如英语十四行诗《晚香玉》、汉英诗歌《荞麦花开》、《紫荆花》、英语俳句《枯萎的玫瑰》之外，以女性的敏感感知自然界的花开花谢、鸟吟虫鸣等，表现出拿捏自如的女性生命纤细本能外，更多的诗歌几乎尽量避开、主动突破了女性诗歌特征，展现出了大开大阖、不拘一格的恢弘气象，成为一个不带性别的真正的"诗人"。在她的诗思里，小到阳台上晾晒内裤的小柔情，行旅之夜及深夜键盘前的思念之情，再到重温羊肠小道和追念大学友情的爽朗豪迈之情，及对故乡一草一木的深深依恋之情，大到侧写河南水灾、新冠疫情，直至正面叙写国际恐怖主义等的人文大情怀……对大自然花草、星月、鸟虫的铺叙，对诗人形象的描写和心理的描摹，更多的，对所见所感的世间万物、社会万象，都能直接拿来落在笔下。

苏菲的英汉双语诗歌原创，是一种诗思自然的语言的流露，轻快爽朗，诗如其人。自自然然，不做作，不勉强。和很多熟读西方诗歌的翻译家不同，苏菲除了将西方的英语诗歌以及其它语种转化成英语的诗歌翻译成汉语诗歌之外，也会读其他翻译家翻译成汉语的外国诗歌，但却没有留下任何国内西方译本那种遣词生硬、故作玄奥的痕迹，写作姿态也非常轻松裕如。

或许和她外向开朗的性格有关，她写诗的灵感多采撷于一事一物，所感所闻；她喜欢按照她客观的所见所闻直接落实到笔端，还原万事万物的本原面目，而不是沉吟良久后，从心中投射出的形象去虚构和美化。她关注周身外界多于关注自身，注重事物的客观描摹重于自身生命体验。因此，她的诗歌总体给人就是一种爽朗明快、轻松自在的感觉。

当然，苏菲也有自己的生命体验，没有生命体验是不可能对一事一物产生深厚的热爱、依恋感情的。她对故乡的热爱，对大学友情的缅怀以及对爱情的体验，不知不觉间早已反射到她叙写的情境中，比如苏菲原创英汉诗歌故乡诗歌系列的《苏菲走过的羊肠小道》《野樱桃花》，写大学情谊的《这三天，啥也不想干》《邂逅十字路——致瑞洁》，写爱情体验的《枯萎的玫瑰》。其中《枯萎的玫瑰》一首，没有爱的融入，就没有满室的"芳香四溢"，那是爱情的味道。但是所有的生命体验，在苏菲的诗里，都巧妙契合到轻快、自然的叙写节奏中，让人容易淡忘这背后殷殷的情怀。

苏菲的英汉双语诗歌原创，总体上是向外的、明快的诗歌。不过随着所处城市、环境、心境的改变，苏菲诗歌对写作素材的敏锐度和诗歌颜色、格调都随之变化。苏菲北京系列诗歌，格调阴郁低沉，当时身心奔波，显得内心动荡而焦虑；苏菲故乡系列诗歌，诗歌色彩缤纷、格调明快亮丽，点点滴滴洋溢着对故乡的挚爱之情；小谷围诗歌系列，显得沉着自如，内容丰富多样，格调也趋于优裕平缓，写作的视野放得更开，诗思的触发点也更加成熟，或纤细或宏大。

苏菲很多诗的创作语言是英语，尤其是苏菲英语十四行诗，讲究英语十四行诗的五步抑扬格，这是她写作难度最大的诗歌，也是她写作最有挑战性的诗歌。这些英语诗歌翻译成汉语之后，汉语诗歌文本和英语诗歌文本之间会形成一定的阅读反差。关于这一点，我还没有资格来评论，有待研究翻译比较的学者来研究、来比较和解读。

2023-09-30 中国广州

From The Dew To The Stream, Poetry Is Flowing Out Naturally

— A Review On Sophy Chen's First Original E-C Poetry Collection A Wizened Rose

[China] Dazang Chen

Sophy Chen's Original English and Chinese Poetry Collection A Wizened Rose, its poetry writing spans 11 years, a very large time span. It is not an easy thing to evaluate Sophy Chen's Original E-C Poetry. As the person closest to her, I am most familiar with her writing and poetry. Over the years, her original English and Chinese bilingual poetry has matured and enriched continuously, transforming from the dewdrop on the flawless English sonnet "Tuberose" into a stream that runs towards the real poetry ocean. As a true poet, she has gradually become mature, calm and even atmospheric, which cannot be said in a few words.

First of all, Sophy Chen's Original English and Chinese Poetry shows the diversity of style and subject matter, and shows the basic characteristics of a mature "poet". It can be said that from the very beginning, except for a few of her poems, such as English sonnets Tuberose, Chinese and English poems, Buckwheat Flowers Blooming and Bauhinia and English Haiku A Wizened Rose, her poems used the sensitivity of women to perceive the flowers blooming and falling in nature, birds singing and insects singing, etc., showing the delicate instinct of female life, and her more poems have almost avoided and actively broke through the characteristics of female poetry, showing a big opening, eclectic grand atmosphere, and becoming a real "poet" without gender. In her poetry, from the small tenderness of drying underwear on the balcony, to the missing feelings in the night of travel and in front of the keyboard in deep night, to the refreshing and magnificent feelings of revisiting the narrow path and recalling the friendship of the university, to the deep love to the grass and trees of the hometown, to the profile of the flood of Henan and the novel coronavirus epidemic, to the positive description of international terrorism and other humanistic feelings... The description of nature flowers and plants, stars and moons, birds and insects, the description of the poet's image and psychology, and more, all the things in the world and social phenomena seen and felt can be directly used to fall into the pen.

Sophy Chen's Original English and Chinese Bilingual Poetry is, a kind of poetic reflection of natural language, light and bright, and her poetry is just like her. It's natural, not pretentious, and not forced. Unlike many translators who are familiar with Western poetry, in addition to translate Western English poetry into Chinese and English poetry translated from other languages into Chinese, Sophy Chen also reads foreign poetry translated into Chinese by other translators, but in her poems there is no trace of the blunt and mysterious words of the domestic Western translation, and her writing posture is very smooth and relaxed. Perhaps it is related to her outgoing and cheerful personality, and her inspiration for writing poems is mostly gathered from one thing or one person, or what she sees or what she feels. She likes to directly write what she has seen and heard in accordance with her objective, restoring the original face of everything, rather than imagining and beautifying the image projected from her mind after a long time. She pays more attention to the outside world than herself, and focuses on the objective depiction of things than her own life experience. Therefore, her poetry generally gives people a kind of refreshing and relaxed feeling.

Of course, Sophy Chen also has her own life experience, and without life experience, it is impossible to have deep love and attachment to one thing. Her love for hometown, the memory of college friendship and the experience of love, have already unconsciously reflected in her narrative situation, such as Sophy Chen's Original E-C Hometown Poetry Series"The Narrow Path Walked By Sophy Chen", "Wild Cherry Blossoms", and her university friendship "In These Three Days, I Don't Want to Do Anything" and "We Met on a Cross Road —To Ruijie" and love experience "A Wizened Rose". Among them, the poem "A Wizened Rose", if there is no love involved, there is no "fragrance overflowing" in the room, and that is the taste of love. However, all life experiences, in Sophy Chen poems, are cleverly fitted into the light and natural narrative rhythm, making people easy to forget the warm feelings behind this.

Sophy Chen's English and Chinese Bilingual Poems are generally outward and bright. However, with the change of city and environment of her living and her mood, the sensitivity of her poetry writing material, the color of her poetry and style of her poetry have been changing. Sophy Chen's Beijing Poetry Series, is in the gloomy and low style, and at that time, in rush of her body and mind, her poems appear her inner turmoil and anxiety; Sophy Chen's Hometown Poetry Series, is colorful in bright and beautiful style, and the dribs and drabs of her poems are filled with her love of hometown; Sophy Chen's Xiaoguwei Island Poetry Series appears calm and free, rich and diverse in content, and tends to be in a gentle and smooth style, and the vision of writing is more open, and the trigger point of poetry is more mature, or slim or grand.

Many poems of Sophy Chen are written in English, especially Sophy Chen's English Sonnets, which emphasize the iambic pentameter of English sonnets, and which is her most difficult poems writing, and also her most challenging poems writing. After these English poems are translated into Chinese, there will be a certain reading contrast between Chinese poetry text and English poetry text. On this point, I am not qualified to comment, and it is waiting for scholars who study translation comparison to study, compare and interpret.

Dazang Chen 2023-09-30, Guangzhou, China

Translated by Sophy Chen, 2023-10-01, Guangzhou, China.

Poems From Sophy Chen's Original E-C Poetry Beijing Poetry Series

苏菲原创英汉诗歌
北京诗歌系列节选

Haiku

A Wizened Rose

On my desk, a white rose

Wizened, in a black vase

But still emanates its fragrance

2012-11-7 Yanjiao Beijing, China

俳句

枯萎的玫瑰

桌上，黑花瓶

一支白玫瑰，枯萎

仍芳香四溢

二零一二年十一月七日 北京 燕郊

北京的月

又是一年
中秋夜

这里是北京
喧嚣的都市
望不断的是故乡的月
星星点点

目光所及的
是那
摩天大楼闪闪的霓虹
听不完的是汽车声声

夹裹在摩天大厦
之间的这轮满月
淹没在
人类的霓虹灯里
凄清而迷茫

23:11 2012-9-29 北二外 中国北京

The Moon In Beijing

It is the Mid-Autumn night
Of another year

This is Beijing
A bustling capital city
What can't be looking constantly is the moon of hometown
Stars in tinny spots

As far as the eyes can see
Are
The neon lights of skyscrapers
What I can't stop listening to is the noise of cars

This full moon
Wrapped between the skyscrapers
Is drown in
The neon lights of humans
Sad and confused

23:11 2012-9-29, Beijing International Studies University，Beijing, China

C-E Translated by Sophy Chen 2023-08-06 Guangzhou, China

失 眠

月光透过天窗
撒了一地……

不知是两杯咖啡的威力
还是黄昏的小憩

夜已深沉
一年的旧事如滔滔江水
奔涌而来

似乎有惊涛骇浪
拍打着我的窗

思维在枕上辗转
却无法预知下一刻
梦将游向何方

3:30 2012-11-26　北京 燕郊

Sleeplessness

Moonlight through the window
Is spreading on the ground...

I don't know it's the power of two cups of coffee
Or an evening nap

It's in deep night
A year's old story as if a surging river
That rushes towards me

It seems like the stormy seas which
Is flapping on my window

Though my mind is tossing on the pillow
I can not predict the next moment
Where my dream will swim to

3:30 2012-11-26 Yanjiao Beijing, China

C-E Translated by Sophy Chen 2018-07-06 Guangzhou, China

Poems From Sophy Chen's Original E-C Poetry Hometown Poetry Series

苏菲原创英汉诗歌 故乡诗歌系列节选

荞麦花开

秋高气爽，仰头望去
一湾压倒式的梯田
彩蝶纷纷，荞麦花开得正浓
成群的蜜蜂在花间低吟

蜜蜂和彩蝶铸成的花海
自然赋予它无尽的芬芳

午后若想打个小盹，去花海吧
仰面躺下，小伙伴千呼万唤
也寻你不着，甜甜地做神仙美梦

此时，时光如若重返
我便携了心底的诗行
在九月的清晨出发
回到花海深处，彩蝶曼舞
蜜蜂低唱，沐浴荞麦芬芳

爸爸说现在退耕还林了
荞麦花开时节是无边的林海
一阵松涛脆响，一股松香袭来
仰头望去，山尖上云雾缭绕

2013-2-27 中国广州

Buckwheat Flowers Blooming

The autumn sky is clean and air is crisp. Looking upward
In a bay of overwhelming terraces
Butterflies are one after another, buckwheat flowers flourishing
And swarms of bees humming among the flowers

Bees and butterflies make the sea of flowers
Nature gives it the endless fragrance

If you want to take a nap in the afternoon, go to the flowers
Lie on your back, and let your small partners call you a great many times
Yet can not find you, then you just do your immortal sweet dreams

At the moment, if the time were back
I would take my poetry at the bottom of my heart
Start in an early morning of September
Go back to the depths of flowers, with butterflies flying
Bees humming and buckwheat fragrance bathing

My father says it's been returning farmlands to forests
In the buckwheat flowers blooming season it's a sea of boundless woodlands
After the soughing of the wind in the pine trees, a stream of rosin hit
Looking upward, it's mist-shrouded on mountain tops

2013-2-27 Guangzhou, China
C-E Translated by Sophy Chen 2015-03-01

苏菲走过的羊肠小道

上初中的时候，天天走
那时，你走，我也走
人来人往，你迎面走来
我侧身给你让路 ——
20 年后的今夜，此时
这条羊肠小道，被雨水
彻底浸溶，一脚踩上去
鞋子便陷进去半截
脚下打滑，你要攀着
两旁的小灌木甚至是荒草
缓缓上行 ……
街坊里借来的雨伞
哪里听你的？
在你手里肆意狂舞
一不小心，手一松劲
它便挣脱去数百步远
你便黑灯瞎火地去追
—— 瞧，那就是自己过去的影子
翻过这座山，转上几道弯
就到家了
上初中的时候，天天走
头顶着月亮，耳边松涛回响
时不时，夜鸟叫上几声
从林子里惊飞 ——
今夜有雨，我没听见鸟叫
唯有雨声，松涛声

脚下荒草发出的噌噌声
翻过这座山，转过几道弯
就到家了
真的，家并不远 ……

2017-02-07 陕西略阳 三岔子

（诗人注：现在几乎家家户户都买了摩托车和小汽车，这条小路走的人
越来越少，几乎废弃了，在大家的劝诫声中，我再次踏上了这条小路，
想看看是不是老眼昏花了，就走不得这羊肠小道了）

The Narrow Path Walked

When I was in junior high school, it was walked every day
At that time, you walked and I walked too
People, going and coming, you were coming towards me
I sidled out of your way —
20 years later tonight, right now
This narrow path, soaked by the rain
Thoroughly and when you step on it
Your shoes will be sunk in half of it
Because of feet slipping, you have to climb
Small shrubs and even grass on both sides of path
Creeping up
The umbrella borrowed from the neighborhood
Where does it listen to you?
Is dancing wildly in your hands
If you're in a careless move, or in a loose hand
It'll break free and go hundreds of paces away
You have to go after it in the dark
— See, that's a shadow of my past
Go over the hill, around a few corners
We'll be home
When I was in junior high school, I walked every day
The moon is overhead, the pine waves echo in my ears
From time to time, the night birds call several times
Flying out of the woods —
It's raining tonight, and I didn't hear the birds calling
Nothing but the sound of rain, the sound of pines

The sound of the grass zooming under feet
Over the hill, around a few corners
We'll be home
Really, home is not far...

2017-02-07 Sanchazi, Lueyang, Shaanxi
Translated By Sophy Chen 2023-08-10 Guangzhou, China

(Poet's Notes: Now almost every family has bought motorcycles and cars, so this narrow path was walked by less and less people, almost abandoned, and in everyone's advice, I once again set feet on this path, and I want to see if my eyes have turned so dimly, I can not walk this small path again)

我将用什么来挽救你，记忆中的绝美

—— 将以此诗献给已故的初高中同学、好友 汪澜

这次回来，是被那朵娇艳似火，却突然
调零的花骨朵从睡梦中硬生生地惊醒的
内心的余悸长久不能平息
它不断地逼迫自己的内心
再不回去 ——
有可能，再也见不到你想见的人！
再不回去 ——
有可能，再也看不到记忆中的风景！
甚至，惧怕再也吃不到家乡的味道！
看，你这朵强行调落的花骨朵
看，这马上就要被拆除的嘉陵古桥
对了，还有已经迁移的略阳一中
还有，改了高速，记忆中的老路
都已经血肉模糊，在大脑里渐行渐远
亦或是诞生苏菲，诞生《晚香玉》的小木屋
都岌岌可危，屋瓦破旧，椽梁朽败，
频临坍塌，或许旧时的物、事、人、非、
都将在生命里永远消亡 ……
我将用什么来挽救你，记忆中的绝美
你说、图片、文字、还是诗歌？！

2017/10/15　中国广州，小谷围岛

What Will I Use to Save You, The Beauty of Memory

— I Dedicate This Poem to Deceased WANG LAN My Middle & High School Classmate & Friend

This time I can come back, because I was waken up abruptly from the sleep
By the flower delicate and bright as fire, but suddenly fallen down
The lingering palpitations in my heart can not be calmed for a long time
It's constantly pushing my heart
If I do not go back now —
It is possible that I'll never see the person I want to see again!
If I do not go back now —
It is possible that I can not see the scenery in my memory!
Even, I fear that I'll never eat the taste of home again!
Look, you're the flower who was forced to fall down
Look, this is the Ancient Jialing Bridge that will be demolished soon
By the way, there is also the already relocated Lue Yang First High School
Also, the old highway from memory, changing into the High Speed Way
It's all in a bloody blur, and it's fading away in my brain
Or the cabin where Sophy Chen was born, where Tuberose was born
It's all crumbling, the tiles are worn out, the rafters are decaying,
Nearly all will collapse, perhaps the past things, stories, people, value of right and wrong,
Will perish forever in life...
What will I use to save you, the beauty of memory
What do you love, pictures, words, or poetry? !

2017/10/15 Guangzhou, Xiao Guwei Island, China

C-E Translated into English by Sophy Chen 2023-08-07 Guangzhou, China

一颗奇异的星星

2020 的今天，都已经立春了
十五也过了，都十六了
但还是异常的寒冷窒息
不准人走动，都统统窝在家里
刚发了一组译诗，一撩棉门帘
突然发现正西方一颗大星星
不但大的出奇，还亮的出奇
山里长大的经验和记忆告诉我
没见过这么大，这么亮的星星
它像极了山尖上竖起的大灯盏
光芒四射，白里泛着红光
我急忙拿了相机，很遗憾
即便是长焦镜头，也没能留住它
突然有人高喊：那是灾星
灾星还是福星，我还没反应过来
它便滚落山崖去了……

2020-02-09 21:30 三岔子 苏菲汉英诗歌原创

A Strange Star

Today in 2020, the Beginning of Spring has already past
The 15th day of the first month of lunar year has already past
And it is the 16th day but still unusually cold and suffocating
No one is allowed to go out to meet people so all people are at home
Just publishing a group of translated poems and lifting cotton door curtain
I suddenly found a big star in the west sky
Not only surprisingly big, but also surprisingly bright
The experience and memories of growing up in the mountains tell me
I've never seen such a big, such a bright star
It looks like a big lamp on the top of mountain
Radiating brilliant light, with white light in red glow
I took the camera in a hurry, but it is a pity
Even the telephoto lens failed to keep it
Suddenly someone shouted loudly: it is a disaster star
A disaster star or a blessing star, I haven't responded yet
It fell off the cliff ...

2020-02-09 21:30 Sanchazi Sophy Chen's Original C-E Poetry

原来呀，月亮就藏在冷冷的山崖边

昨夜是正月十五，夜里加班翻译
山乡的月亮明亮，旷远
午夜寒意侵入骨髓，没好好欣赏
今夜正月十六，月亮应该最圆了
却突然发现月亮竟然没有出来
望了望屋顶，峡谷的四面山崖
都不见月亮的影儿，月亮哪里去了
难道十六的月亮还被乌云遮住了
转身的瞬间，突然发现谷间东边
黑黢黢的山崖上泛起浅浅的光晕
光晕越来越强，直到
山崖上树影稀疏可见，慢慢地
月儿从树影里泛起朦胧的光影，光影
越来越强，越来越大，越来越清晰
直到整个身子掩映在婆娑的树影里
如果你换个角度欣赏，月亮呀
它已唯美地挂在山坳树梢儿上了
那冷清，顿觉旷谷间寒意深浓 ……
原来呀，月亮就藏在冷冷的山崖边

2020-02-09 22:22 三岔子 苏菲汉英诗歌原创

It Turns Out That The Moon Is Hidden By The Cold Cliff

Last night , it was the 15th day of the first month of lunar year, I translated
poems overtime at night
In the mountain village the moon is bright and distant
The chill invaded my bone marrow at midnight, so I did not appreciate it
Tonight it is the 16th day of the first month of lunar year and the moon should
be round the most
But I suddenly found out that the moon didn't come out
Looking over the roof and the four sides of the canyon
There is no shadow of the moon, where is the moon
Is the moon of the 16th day of the first month of lunar year covered by dark clouds
The moment when I turned around, I suddenly found in the east of canyon
There was a shallow halo on the black cliff of it
The halo is getting stronger and stronger, till
On the cliff the shadow of the trees can be seen sparsely, slowly
The moon rose a dim light shadow from the shadows of the trees, the light shadow
Is getting stronger and stronger, bigger and bigger, and clearer and clearer
Until its whole body is appearing in the dancing tree shadows
If you look at it from another angle, the moon oh
It hangs beautifully on the treetop of hillside
To see its cold and cheerless looking, I suddenly felt deep cold between the canyon ...
It turns out that the moon is hidden by the cold cliff

2020-02-09 22:22 Sanchazi, Sophy Chen's Original C-E Poetry

溪荪

溪荪，你翠绿的叶子是家门口最最盛大的绿意
当冬天遍野枯黄，你们便成了眼前唯一的绿意
每次回来几乎都是冬天，万物都枯萎沉寂不语
唯有溪荪给我大片大片一望无际的绿意无论是
凄厉的冬雨还是大雪纷纷，都无法阻挡你的绿
突然想起你们夏天的倩影，倒映在溪流的影子
现在几乎记不准确，你们开花的时节了，不过
不过记忆里那个时候，你们最最引人注目的是
那淡蓝色的碎花，在溪流里掩映，往往都会有
水喜鹊在花间掠过，水喜鹊和溪荪花定是绝配
那一瞬间的美，只有记忆可以让你们永恒绝美

2020-02-09 22:58 三岔子 苏菲汉英诗歌原创

Siberian Iris

Siberian Iris, your green leaves are the most grand green in front of my house
When winter is yellow withering, you become the only green in front of me
Every time when I came back, it is almost winter, everything is withered and silent
Only Siberian Iris give me a vast expanse of green as far as the eyes can see
Whether it is in stern winter rain or heavy snow, it can not stop your green
Suddenly I thought of your summer shadow, the shadow reflected in the stream
Now I can hardly remember exactly what season you are flowering
But in my memory at the time, the most striking thing about you was
The blue small flowers set each other off in the stream, there are always water magpies
Sliding over in the flowers, water magpies and the flowers are surely a good match
The beauty of that moment, only memory can make you beautiful forever

2020-02-09 22:58 Sanchazi Sophy Chen's Original C-E Poetry

迎春花开了

按照往年的惯例，今天是 2 月 14 日
情人节，他总会买两三只白玫瑰回来
可现到哪里买玫瑰呢！都被困在家里

穷乡僻壤，哪有卖花的，又不准出门
公交停了，出租停了，滴滴停了，私家车也 …
步行赶集的人回来说，村口焊了铁门
对了，快递也停了，网上也买不成了！

突然想起太爷爷坟头的迎春花
想必它们该开放了吧！拿了照相机
踩着毛路路上的枯叶荒草，爬了一面坡
等到全身发热了，也终于到了

坟头杂草横生，几只光秃秃，翠绿的
迎春花枝丫格外醒目，稀疏的花蕾含苞欲放
竟然有一朵小碎花破蕾而出
淡黄色小碎花儿在荒草堆里，神气十足

我们终于缓了一口气 …..
在这阴冷，干枯，闭塞，窒息的空气里
迎春花终于开了，开在这个没有玫瑰的春天 ……

2020-02-14 21:58 三岔子 苏菲汉英诗歌原创

Winter Jasmine Is Blossoming

According to the practice of previous years, today is February 14
The Valentine's Day, he always buys two or three white roses
But now where can we buy roses? All people are trapped at home

In the remote countryside, no one sells flowers and all people are not
allowed to go out
Bus stops, taxi stops, Didi stops, and private cars also...
People who walked to market came back and said village gate was welded
with iron gates
By the way, the express delivery has also stopped so we cannot buy online either!

Suddenly I remembered the winter jasmine on my great-grandfather's grave
Presumably they should be blossoming! I took my camera
Stepping on dead leaves and dry weeds of sloping road, up a big slope
And when we feel hot, we finally arrives at the grave

Weeds on head of the grave, several bare and verdant
Winter jasmine branches are particularly eye-catching, and their sparse
buds are budding
Unexpectedly there is a small flower bursting out of the bud
The yellowish small flower is full of energy in the haystack

We finally took a sigh of relief ...
In this cold, dry, blocking, and suffocating air
The winter jasmine is finally blooming and blooming in this no roses spring

2020-02-14 21:58 Sanchazi   Sophy Chen's Original C-E Poetry

瘦溪水

故乡的溪水，瘦溪水，小时候并不觉得它们瘦
特别是夏天戏水、石头缝里抓螃蟹
溪水潭里捉蚂蚱什么的，可就是没有小鱼小虾
据说是溪水太瘦，瘦得连鱼虾都不生长的
近几年回来，都是过年，突然发现它们越发瘦了
瘦得几乎听不见流水声，甚至看不见水在流了
就算是你上山捡柴、地里刨土、除草回来
半路上想喘喘气、歇歇脚、洗洗手什么的
都几乎无法聚集一小潭细水来，洗洗弄脏的手脸了
不知道是由于大量引水，还是山里采矿的原因
竟然让它们这般的瘦弱了 —— 几代人饮用的山泉水
就这样一瘦，再瘦，再再瘦，瘦得几近干涸了

2020-02-29 11:50 中国 三岔子 苏菲汉英诗歌原创

Thin Stream

Streams in my hometown, thin streams, I did not think they were thin when I
was young
Especially playing, catching crabs in the cracks of stones in summer or catching
The water grasshoppers or something in the stream pool, but no small fishes
and shrimps
It is said that the stream is so thin that it does not even grow fishes and shrimps
In recent years, I'm always back for Lunar New Year and suddenly I find
they're getting thinner
I can narely hear the sound of running water, or even see the water flowing
Even if you want to have a breath, take a break, wash your hands or
something on the way back
After collectting wood from the mountain, and digging earth and weeds in fields
You could hardly gather a small water hole to wash your soiled hands and face
I don't know if it's due to a large amount of water diversion or mining in mountains
They've made them so thin and the mountain springs for generations's drinking
Like this, so thin, thinner, thinner, and thinner, and nearly drained

2020-02-29 11:50 Sanchazi, China, Sophy Chen's Original C-E Poetry

野樱桃花

第一场春雨过后，最最盛大的花海
是门前四面山上满山遍野的野樱桃花
它们穿越漫漫寒冬，默默的等待
从粉色的花苞儿，到齐火火如雪绽放飘飞
你极目远眺，那绽放的圣洁花海
总给你无限的憧憬和向往
长焦镜头也无法穷尽它们的圣洁
好多时候，你会忍不住穿越
无数荆棘丛林，穿行在纷飞的花海
当小蜜蜂在耳边嗡嗡不停，此时
你真的徜徉花海了，如果有幸，你会偶遇
一两只鸟儿在花间啄食，小小一支花儿
便可让它们细细的爪子稳稳倒挂着
等满山遍野，满树满树挂满红玛瑙的季节
那该是它们多丰盛的午餐呀！

2020-03-11　三岔子　苏菲汉英诗歌原创

Wild Cherry Blossoms

After the first spring rain, the most magnificent sea of blossoms
Is the wild cherry blossoms on mountains of all sides of the door
They travel through the slow winter, waiting silently
From pink buds to blooming like snow
When you look far away, the blooming sea of holy blossoms
Always give you the unlimited longing and yearning
Telephoto lenses can't exhaust their holiness either
Many times, you can't help to cross
The countless bushes of thorns, walking through the sea of blossoms
When the little bee buzzes in the ear, at this moment
You're really wandering in the sea of blossoms, if you're lucky, you'll come across
One or two birds hunting among the flowers, a small branch of flowers
Can make their thin claws hang upside down
When the season, trees full of red agates on all mountains
That should be their great lunch!

2020-03-11 Sanchazi Sophy Chen's Original Chinese-English Poetry

Poems From Sophy Chen's Original English Sonnets

苏菲原创 英语十四行诗节选

Sophy Chen's English Sonnet 1

After Ten Years

— This is the first sonnet I wrote in English and I wish it is a very good beginning

English language is not my mother tone
In English, I wrote a poem to you ten years ago
That's the first English poem I wrote, as time goes on
I actually didn't know why I did so

You, on the video today when I met
It is ten years after I see you again
You may not know why after ten years
Your eyes are still sharp as yours of the past

When you gave English class to your students
As ten years ago you're still vigorous
In a foreign language, your confidence
Are always obviously shown in your class

I'm writing you the poem after ten years
Well, I feel, some wrinkles, on your face

2013-04-07 in Xiao Guwei Island, China

苏菲英语十四行诗 之一

十年之后

—— 这是我第一首英语十四行诗，希望是个良好的开端

英语，这门语言，它并不是我的母语
十年之前，我用英语给你，写了一首诗
那是我写的第一首，英语诗，时光飞逝
其实，我不知道，为什么，给你写诗

今天，遇见你的时候，你在视频里
我们，再次相遇，这已是，十年之后
你可能，不知道，为什么，十年之后
你的双眼，依然锐利，依然，犹如当年

当你给，学生，上英语课的时候
正如十年之前，你依然，生机勃勃
在一门外语里，你的，强势的自信
总在，课堂上，明显的，自然流露

十年之后，我正在给你写，这首诗
然而，我感觉，你的脸颊，些许皱纹

2013-04-07 中国小谷围岛

苏菲英译汉 2021－04－20 中国小谷围岛

Sophy Chen's English Sonnet 3

Tuberose

As I was young my mom planted some flowers
In front of our old wooden house in springs
In my memory they were peony, China rose…
But what I loved the most was the tuberose

In summer night it's a nice time to me
You could sit in yard to listen the night birds
Singing on cliffs, insects singing in bushes
And look at the moon moving in night skies

However, while your heart was beating at pace
With insects singing and in the sudden
From nowhere floating a ray of fragrance
In the moon a bunch of tuberose blossoms

As these flowers always bloom in moon nights
Your great poem may be living in its fragrance

2013-10-05   In China

苏菲英语十四行诗 之三

晚香玉

小的时候，我家木屋门前
春天，妈妈总会种些花儿
记忆深处有牡丹，有月季……
我最喜欢的花，是晚香玉

夏日的夜晚，是最美好的
你坐在院子里，听夜鸟们
在悬崖歌唱，虫儿们低吟
看月牙儿，在夜空里流转

当你的心弦，和着虫儿们
的低吟节律地律动，突然
从哪里，飘来一缕缕芬芳
月光下，晚香玉次第绽放

这花儿总在，这月夜开放
你不朽诗篇，芬芳里滋长

2013 年 10 月 5 日 中国广州

（苏菲原创英汉对照诗歌）

Sophy Chen's English Sonnet 4

We Met on a Cross Road

— To Ruijie

I've searched you on web by all your key words
Thousands of times I failed with great sadness
By accident you appeared in my dream
Last night we met on our way to classroom

But I didn't know which University it was
It looks like around mountains, trees and cliffs
As if our departure we met on a cross road
With smile in vain at each other we looked

"Where are you going to?" unnaturally I asked
"On my way to be a linguist" You said
"I'd like to be a poet" eagerly I said
With long hair dancing in the wind you nodded

Suddenly I was woken by women gossiping
Out side of window with some dogs barking

2013-10-10 In Guangzhou, China

苏菲英语十四行诗 之四

邂逅十字路

—— 致瑞洁

网上，搜遍了你的关键词
数千次杳无踪迹，我心伤
突然与我梦里，出来相见
昨夜去教室偶然路上碰见

我不知道，那是哪家大学
它被群山、悬崖密林围绕
仿佛，你我在十字路道别
相视微笑，心有万般无奈

"去哪里？"我拘谨地问
"去语言学家的路"你说
"我要作诗人"我急切地
你点头，长发，风中飘舞

突然，被闲妇家常，惊醒
窗外，几条狗，汪汪不停

2013-10-10 中国广州

（2104-10-01 苏菲 英译汉 中国广州）

Sophy Chen's English Sonnet 12

As if I'd Fallen in Its Waves

As I was back to my country crossing the bridge
The Jialing River bathing in sun rising always
I would think of you by leaning on its railings
As if I'd fallen in its waves in one thousand years

If I did not cross it I'd see you every day
I'd touch your smile, your lady killer eyes
I thought I'd rather touch your eyes forever
You may not know the bridge I suffered so

In that year I must pass the ancient bridge
As soon as possible, for if I did not cross it
I was quite sure I would drop into the river
And disappear without any echoes forever

The bridge has been damaging almost for 20 years
Where is your charming eyes, the bridge knows

2014-03-11 In Guangzhou China

仿若跌入你的浪涛

每次回故乡，穿过这古桥
嘉陵江沐浴，初升的太阳
斜倚栏杆，我总会想起你
仿若跌入你的浪涛已千年

不过这桥，会天天见到你
触到你的笑容，心醉的眼
我想我会永远触着你的眼
你不知这桥，我饱尝泪水

那年，我必须跨过这古桥
越快越好，如果不过这桥
我深信，我定然深陷江涛
消失，永远没有任何回响

20 年来，这桥遭受着毁损
哪有你迷人的眼，桥知道？

2014 年 3 月 11 日，中国广州

（2016-04-13 苏菲 英译汉 中国广州）

Poems From Sophy Chen's Original E-C Poetry
Xiaoguwei Island Poetry Series

苏菲原创英汉诗歌
小谷围岛诗歌系列节选

夜

52

夜，在火车的摇移中侵入漫长，
你在摇移中进入梦乡；
你靠着的不是冰冷的车窗，
是他坚实的臂膀。

Sophy Chen   2011-06-10 广州 - 西安火车上

Night

53

The night, moves into the endlessness with moving and shaking of the train

You're going to sleep with its moving and shaking

What you're leaning is not the cold window of the train

But his strong arms

Sophy Chen 2011-06-10 On the train from Guangzhou to Xian

C-E Translated by Sophy Chen 2018-06-10

你不睡，我不敢入眠

睡吧，亲爱的，
你不睡，我不敢入眠。

睡吧，远方的你，
夜已沉静，
再无汽车的轰轰声
行人的脚步声
只留下
键盘的敲打声
在恍惚，迷离里
回响 .....
回响 ......

睡吧，亲爱的，
你不睡，我不敢入眠。

苏菲汉英诗歌原创 凌晨 3:33 2011-11-29
广外翰林书苑

You Do Not Sleep, And I Dare Not Sleep

Sleep, my dear
You do not sleep, and I dare not sleep

Sleep, you, far away
It has been quiet
No cars roar any more
No footsteps of pedestrians
Only left
The sound of keyboard
In the mist, and blur
Echoing…
Echoing…

Sleep, my dear
You do not sleep, and I dare not sleep

Sophy Chen's Original Chinese English Poetry
3:33 am 2011-11-29 Han Lin Shu Yuan, Guangdong Foreign Studies &
Trading University

C-E Translated by Sophy Chen 2018-06-08

紫荆花

一草，一木，一花
一世界
羊城的春天
是紫荆花的世界

高大的乔木
粉里透红的花枝凤尾
在二月的柔风里
曼舞，轻歌
惊起落红无数

Sophy Chen 2021-03-03 11:25:56 小谷围岛

Bauhinia

A kind of grass, of wood, of flower
A kind of world
Spring in Yangcheng
Is a world of Bauhinia

On tall trees
Pink red branches as phoenix-tails
In the gentle breeze of February
Are tenderly dancing and singing
With startled flowers falling

Sophy Chen 2021-03-03 11:25:56 in Xiaoguwei Island

两束光的距离……

无论它们再怎么无限靠近，
始终位于两个别样的世界，
从无限中来，到无限中去。

2017-01-08 广州

Distance Between Two Beams of Light

No matter how infinitely they close,

But they're always in two different world,

From infinity to infinity.

2017-01-08 Guangzhou

C-E Translated by Sophy Chen 2018/1/12

满是阳光的味道

在一楼，阳台
被几丛香蕉树常年遮蔽着
很难见到太阳
又是他的小小花样儿
竟让晒不到太阳的底裤
一排排，花花绿绿
花蝴蝶一样
在窗栏上飘飞着！
触手可及，干干爽爽
满是阳光的味道 ......

2021-02-05 00:58 中国广州

Full of the Smell of Sunshine

On the first floor, the balcony

Covered by a few clusters of banana trees all year round

It's hard to see the sun

It's his little trick again

The underpants that can't be exposed to the sun

Rows of colorful flowers

Flower butterflies

Are flying on the window bars!

At my fingertips, dry and cool

Full of the smell of sunshine...

2021-02-05 00:58 Guangzhou, China

母语情结

——波兰诗人扎嘎耶夫斯基印象

国际诗歌奖颁奖现场
室外大雨倾盆
登台领奖前，他总是
正襟危坐表情严肃
等着签名的读者排起长队

大家伸长脖子看他签名
一线落笔，沉默
似乎看不出一丝表情变化
你感受到他
哲学家特有的气质

"Nice to meet you Sir!
Could you sign…? "
我自然的翻开诗集扉页呈上
他一脸茫然，翻译用波兰语
示意之后，他才挥笔
快速签上自己的波兰语大名
然后，默不作声

长达一小时的波兰语受奖词
他恳切殷殷，我们却
如聋子般看着他，等到耳膜
终于灌进一句世界通用语：
"Ladies and Gentlemen"
语调优美，自然，令人欣喜

63

朗诵环节上，他似乎感受到了
观众的茫然与无奈，被迫逼出
一大段流畅的英语开场白……

2014-03-31　中国广州

Mother Tongue Complex

—An Impression of the Polish Poet Adam Zagajewski

In the International Poetry Award site
It rains cats and dogs outside
Before going up on the stage to accept his prize, he always
Straightens his clothes and sits properly with a serious look
Readers line up waiting for his signature

They are craning their necks to look at him to sign
Putting pen to paper with a line, in silence
It seems unable to see a trace of his expression changes
You can feel his
Philosopher's unique qualities

"Nice to meet you Sir!
Could you sign ...?"
I naturally open the title page of the poetry anthology forward
He, bewildered, after his translator
Gave him a sign, quickly swipes
His pen to sign his name in Polish
Then, in silence

In an hour-long polish rewarding speech
He speaks earnestly, but
We look at him as the deaf, until our eardrums
Finally are poured a lingua franca:
"Ladies and Gentlemen"
Beautiful tone, natural, gratifying

65

In the poem reading part, he seems to feel
The daze and helplessness of the audience and then he is forced to squeeze out
A large section of fluent English opening remarks...

2014-03-31 Guangzhou, China

(Published in the "Classics of New Century Poetry" Sophy Day 2014-09-26)

面对恐怖主义，诗歌是一无是处的是处

我 24 小时挂在网上，我更换了所有搜索引擎
所有关键词，在互联网的夹缝里
我嗅见了你的一丝气息
我 48 小时挂在网上，像热锅上的蚂蚁
一次次试图，漫过这热气腾腾的油锅
好看清你的真面目，好让你听见我在哭泣
我 72 小时挂在网上，我飞蛾扑火
一次次试图，越过那幻象中的画屏
好在你面前展现，我最完美的舞姿
好让你看得见，我坠入火海，那永恒的瞬间
我寻遍了整个地球，追寻你的蛛丝马迹
从互联网的缝隙里，我窥见了你的只言片语 ——
面对恐怖主义，诗歌苍白无力
面对恐怖主义，诗歌一无是处
我寻遍了整个宇宙，探求你的缘起缘灭
在宇宙的裂缝里，我窥见了你残留的原代码 ——
面对恐怖主义，诗歌是无力的无力
面对恐怖主义，诗歌是一无是处的是处

2015-11-23 香港，如心铜锣湾海景酒店

Faced With Terrorism, Poetry Is Nothings' Nothing

Have been hung on the line in 24 hours, I replaced all of search engines
And all of key words, and in the internet's cracks
I sniffed your slightest breath
Have been hung on the line in 48 hours, 1, like ants on a hot pan
Again and again trying to, over this steaming pan
In order to see your true colors better, and let you hear me crying
Have been hung on the line in 72 hours, I, like a flying moth darting into the flames
And again and again trying to, over the illusion painted screen
In order to show you my best dancing, in front of you
And let you see my eternal moment, as I fell in the flames
I've searched through the whole earth, following your clues
And from the cracks of internet, I got a glimpse of your few words —
Faced with terrorism, poetry is pale and powerless
Faced with terrorism, poetry is nothing
I've searched through the whole universe, exploring your origin and end
In the cracks of the universe, I got a glimpse of the original code you remained —
Faced with terrorism, poetry is powerless' powerless
Faced with terrorism, poetry is nothings' nothing

2015-11-23, Causeway Bay Harbour View Hotel, Hong Kong

2015-12-02, C-E Translated by Sophy Chen, Xiaoguwei Island, Guangzhou, China

蝉　鸣

住在楼上的时候，除了风声，雨声，
就是一群小孩的哭声，家长呵斥孩子的骂声。

最近有幸搬到地面上，四面窗户，周围绿树环绕，
便奇迹般的听见了，阵阵蝉鸣，
我读英语，他们也读英语！
我一阵平滑的美式英语，调子平缓
激起一阵小小的水波纹，他们的调子也随之
变得轻缓，我一阵大波浪伦敦 BBC 英语
句子重音急速增强 ——
形容词、副词最重，名词、动词次之，
代词、连词弱读，介词一般要吞音。
他们特别贴心，似乎能听懂我的英语
又似乎在模仿我 ——
我停顿，他们停顿，我换气，他们换气
我吐字打个磕，他们也打个磕！
我朗读海明威英文小说《老人与海》
呵！他们也读这个，我朗读 50 次，录制 50 次
他们也是，各 50 次，不离不弃，形影不离！

2016-08-02　中国 小谷围岛

The Song of Cicadas

When I lived the upstairs, apart from the sound of wind and rain,
It was just the crying of a group of kids, and parents yelling at their kids.

Recently I was so lucky to move my room to the ground, surrounded by
four windows and trees,
Miraculously, I heard the song of cicadas,
I read English, they read English too!
I speak the smooth American English in a flat tone
It creates a little ripple of water, and their tune followed
To slow down; I have a big wave in London BBC English
Sentence stress increases rapidly —
Adjectives and adverbs are the most strong, followed by nouns and verbs.
Pronouns, conjunctions are weak, and sounds of prepositions are usually swallowed.
They are so sweet and seem to understand my English
And seem to imitate me —
I pause, they pause, I breathe, they breathe
I make a dent in my words, they make a dent in their words too!
I read Hemingway's English novel "The Old Man And The Sea".
Oh! They read this, too. I read it 50 times, I record it 50 times
So do they, 50 times, inseparable, be always together!

2016-08-02 Xiao Guwei Island, China

C-E Translated by Sophy Chen 2023-08-06 Guangzhou, China

In These Three Days, I Don't Want to Do Anything

— When a person cannot be found, you'll find how wonderful the past life together was

In these three days, I don't want to do anything
I only want to lie in your heat-able brick bed
I don't want to read English
In the morning
I only want to lie in your heat-able brick bed, and look at you making
Chinese pollen tea, no sugar, a cup by a cup, you drink, I drink
Putting more coal!
Mindless of the nice snowflakes outside the cave dwelling
In these three days,
I don't want to write poems
I only want to lie in your heat-able brick bed, and look at you cooking, morning,
The sweet millet porridge for me, with a small plate of self-made pickled vegetable,
Noon, buckwheat noodles, night, mutton soup …
Putting coal again!
Mindless of thick snow and strong wind outside the cave dwelling
In these three days,
I don't want to translate poems
I only want to lie in your heat-able brick bed, and to listen to you tell your love story
Or from time to time, I just boast out
What I have done in English language
Putting more coal again!
Mindless of the heavy snow sealed mountains and blocked the road ahead outside
In these three days,
I really don't want to do anything
I even don't want to teach English, open my computer,

Phone calls, and read short massages in Weibo, or Weixin
Just let the heavy snow sealed mountains and cut down anything which can touch me
One thing that I desperately want to do is to wait and look you cooking
delicious food for me —
Morning, pollen tea, the millet porridge, noon, buckwheat noodles, night,
mutton soup …

2015-04-23 10:16 Xiao Guwei Island, China

这三天，啥也不想干

—— 一个人，只有无法找寻时，才发现相处的时光多么美好

这三天，啥也不想干
只想躺在你那土炕上
清晨
不想读英语
只想躺在你那土炕上，看着你，
做花粉茶，不放糖，一杯，一杯，我喝，你也喝
多加点煤
窑洞外，雪花多美也不管
这三天，
我不想写诗
只想躺在你那土炕上，看着你，
做香喷喷的小米粥，外加一碟你亲手腌制的小咸菜，
中午，荞麦面节节，晚上，羊肉汤 ……
再加点煤
窑洞外，雪再厚，风再大也不管
这三天，
我不想译诗
只想躺在你那土炕上，听你讲述爱情故事
或者，时不时，也自吹自擂
说说自己在英语语言里干了些什么
再多加点煤
窑洞外，大雪封山，阻断前路也不管
这三天，
实在什么也不想干
甚至不想，教授英语、开电脑、

开手机、看，微博，微信
就让大雪封山，切断一切联系
唯有一件，最想，就是，看着你，等着你，做最可口的饭菜 ——
早晨，花粉茶，小米粥，中午，荞麦面节节，晚上，羊肉汤……

（苏菲英汉对照诗歌原创） 2015-04-23 10:16 中国 小谷围岛

I'm Full of Poetry

When I met poet DOC Penpen in Manila
For my WORLD INSPIRATIONAL POET 2018
For our first meeting, of course,
I found he did not have food two days
In Okada Hotel we poets had a coffee,
Cheese and chocolate breakfast together
We talked poems and poets about China
Philippines, and of course, the world
We talked and talked with high spirit
But he was busy for poetry meeting preparation
The welcome dinner in Okada hotel
Outside of window it was a music Spring only for me
In romance,when we all finished our supper
I suddenly found he seemingly did not take food
On seaside, when all poets finished lunch
On a ship restaurant, he was hurry to come
Following a group of cameramen…
I asked " did you take your lunch?"
He always smiled without a word
At night poetry ceremony, when we sat side by side
I couldn't stop me " How about your supper?"
He whispered tenderly in my ear
"I am full of poetry"

2018-09-04 Guangzhou, China

我装满了诗意

和诗人朋朋博士在马尼拉会晤
来领 2018 世界精神诗人奖
当然，这是我们第一次见面
我发现他两天滴水未进
冈田酒店，诗人们一起早餐
喝咖啡、吃奶酪、巧克力
我们谈中国诗歌、中国诗人、菲律宾
诗歌、菲律宾诗人，当然还有世界诗歌和诗人
我们聊呀，聊呀，大家都兴致勃勃
可朋朋正忙着准备诗歌活动
冈田酒店举行的欢迎晚宴
窗外，是专门为苏菲播放的音乐喷泉
好浪漫，当大家吃完晚餐
我突然发现朋朋似乎没吃什么
海边，游轮餐馆里，诗人们都
吃完了午饭，朋朋才匆匆赶来，
身后一群摄像机 ……
我问"吃午饭了吗？"
他总是微笑着，一言不发
晚上的颁奖典礼，我们肩并肩坐着
我无法抗拒自己："吃晚饭了吗？"
他附在我耳边，悄悄声说
"我装满了诗意"

2018-09-04 中国广州

境　界

——至一位中国僧侣行吟诗人

他用一张布布
把自己的书摆在大街上兜售
手里还捏着一两本
行人匆匆而过 ……
他不断给他们引荐解说着
还得盯着无处不在的城管
眼里略显焦虑，但却
萧然而闲然自得
我俩在边上给他充了一天气
广州的年关，虽算不上冷
但不经意略显萧瑟之意
接连几天，我们像是得了
焦虑症，内心煎熬不已
似乎双双回到了萧瑟的旧日

2021-09-22 03:40 苏菲汉英诗歌原创 小谷围岛

Spirituality

——To A Chinese Monk Troubadour

On a piece of cloth he
Is selling his books in the street
A copy or two copies in his hands
Pedestrians hurrying by...
He kept introducing and explaining to them
And also had to keep an eye on the city inspectors who are everywhere
With a little anxiety in his eyes, but
He is quiet and carefree
We are there to give him a bit of encourage in a whole day
At the end of the year in Guangzhou, though it is not cold
But it is a little cold and desolate
For a few days, it seemed like we got
The anxiety, and with the inner torment
It's like we're back to the cold and desolate old days

2021-09-22 03:40 Sophy Chen's C-E Original Poetry Xiaoguwei Island

C-E Translated by Sophy Chen 2023-08-03

沉 默

昨夜微博上看到
郑州大水淹了地铁
沉默？似乎是个营销号
今天自媒体看到
郑州地铁淹到了肩膀
此刻，交感神经不断
抵抗着沉默
翻来覆去睡不着
脑电波玩命地打着圈圈
是继续沉默？
还是相信谣言？

2021-07-23 00:42 苏菲汉英诗歌原创 小谷围岛

Keep Silence

Last night in Weibo, I saw

The subway flooded in Zhengzhou

Keep silence? It looks like a marketing account

Today in a Weichat personal media I saw

The subway flooded up to the shoulders in Zhengzhou

Right now, the sympathetic nerves are pumping

To resist the silence

In tossing and turning I can't sleep

My brain waves are in crazy circles

Shall I remain silent?

Or believe the rumors?

2021-07-23 00:42 Sophy Chen's C-E Original Poetry Xiaoguwei Island

C-E Translated by Sophy Chen in 2023-08-03

你我的圣诞夜

圣诞夜，出去走走！
江滨路，一路灯火阑珊
今天是圣诞夜，也是周日
往年肘碰肘，人山人海
现在只留你我的影子
步履蹒跚 ......

2022-12-25 20:20 中国广州

Christmas Eve For You and Me

In Christmas Eve, we go for a walk!

Along the Riverside Road, the lights are sparking

It's Christmas Eve and also Sunday

In the past, elbows to elbows, the sea of people

But now only your shadow and mine

Are faltering......

2022-12-25 20:20, Guangzhou. China

遥望蛇口夕阳

在深圳湾
海平面被雾霾笼罩着
夕阳略显苍老
三只海鸭逆流而上向我们游来
人们伸长脖子，望向同一个方向
香港蛇口，夕阳西下的地方

人潮涌动，手机，摄像头不断闪动
我几乎找不到一线天
可以留住它的旷世绝美
眼看着，夕阳瞬间被雾霾吞噬
对面的蛇口灯火阑珊！
新月如钩……

呀，起风了！寒气逼人
此刻，没有摘掉的口罩成了
人们真正的庇护

2023-01-24 19:00 中国深圳 深圳湾

（苏菲汉英双语诗歌原创）

Looking At Sun Setting of Shirko

At Shenzhen Bay
The sea is covered by smog
The setting sun appears a bit old looks
Going against the current, three sea ducks are swimming towards us
People are stretching their necks and looking at the same direction
Shirko of Hong Kong, the place, the sun setting

Crowds moving as waves, lights of phones and cameras flashing
I nearly can not find a narrow thin strip of sky
Which can take a photo of its splendid beauty
I just only look at it being swollened by smog at once
At the opposite of the sea, Shirko, lights twinkling!
The moon as a hook......

Ah, wind rising, in chilly air
At this time, the masks that can not be taken down became
The real shelter of people

2023-01-24, 19:00 Shenzhen Bay, Shenzhen China

（The Chinese & English Original Poetry of Sophy Chen）

Sophy Chen's First E-C Original Poetry Collection
苏菲首部英汉诗歌原创集

A Wizened Rose
枯萎的玫瑰

Cophyright© 著作权

Author：Sophy Chen / Lihua Chen
作　者：苏　菲 ／ 陈丽华
Chief Editor：Sophy Chen / Lihua Chen
主　编：苏　菲 ／ 陈丽华

Publisher：Sophy International Translation Publishing House
出版社：苏菲国际翻译出版社
ISBN / 书号：ISBN 978-8-9888271-1-5

Edited And Published："Sophy Poetry & Translation" C-E World Poetry Paper Magazine
编辑出版：《苏菲诗歌 & 翻译》英汉纸质世界诗刊社
Editor：Dazang Chen, Sophy Chen
编　辑：大　藏、苏　菲
Cover Design：Sophy Chen, Dazang Chen
封面设计：苏　菲、大　藏
Layout Design：Dazang Chen
排　版：大　藏

Address：Room 1609, Kowloon Bank, 555, Littleton Road, Mongkok, Kowloon, Hong Kong
通讯地址：香港九龙旺角弥顿道 555 号九龙行 1609 室
Country：[China] HKSAR
国　家：[中国] 香港特区
Folio：210x140 mm
开　本：210x140 毫米
Amount：0001-2000 copies
印　数：0001-2000 册
Edition：First print on Sep 30 2023
版　次：2023 年 9 月 30 日第 1 次印刷
Price：CNY 120　HKD 430　USD 100
定　价：人民币 120 元　港币 430 元　美元 100 元

Tel / 微信电话：0086-18201007874
https://www.sophypoetry.com